2/6

HABITATS OF THE WORLD

MOUNTAINS

ALISON BALLANCE

DOMINIE PRESS
Pearson Learning Group

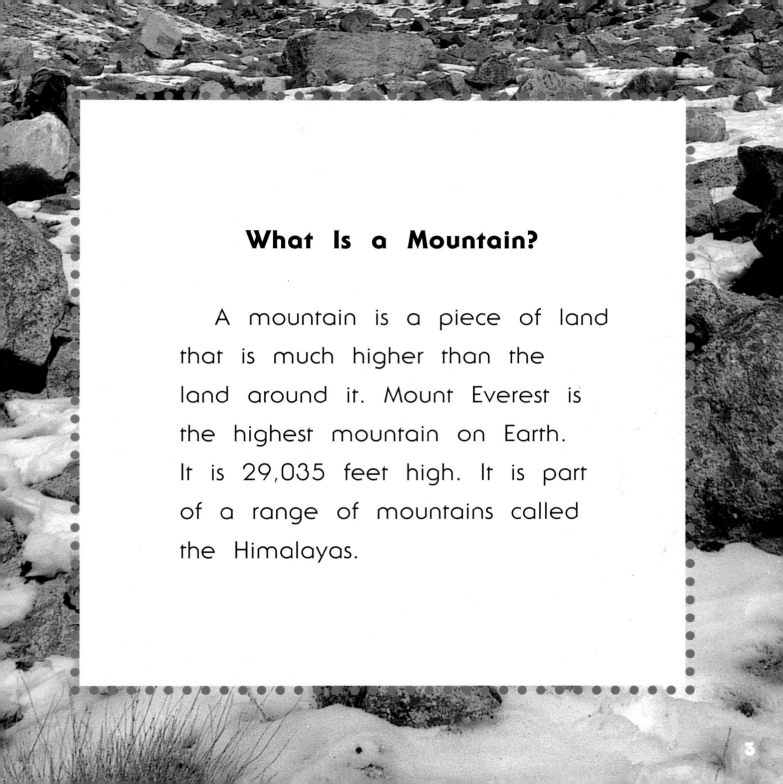

What Is a Mountain?

A mountain is a piece of land that is much higher than the land around it. Mount Everest is the highest mountain on Earth. It is 29,035 feet high. It is part of a range of mountains called the Himalayas.

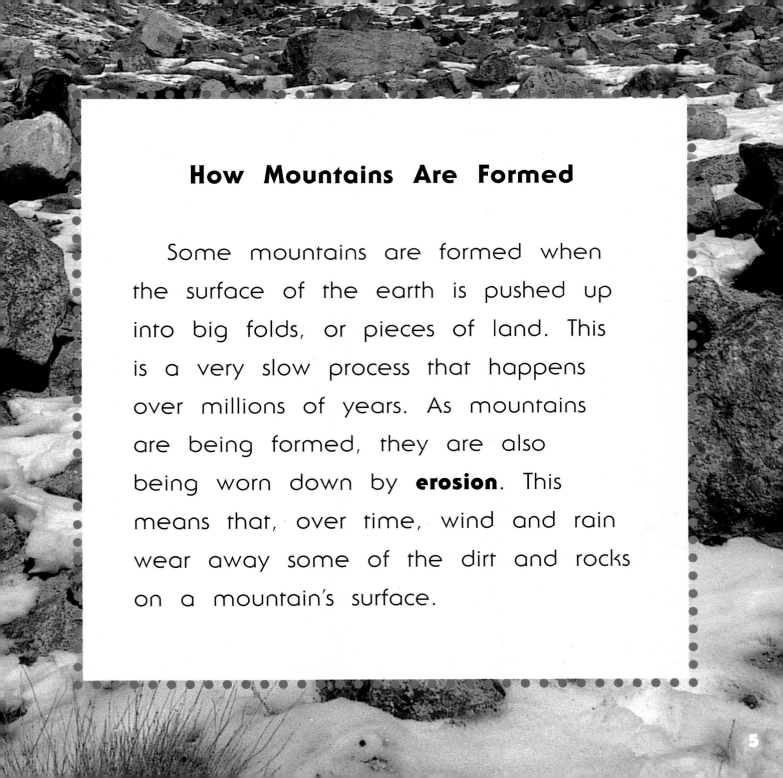

How Mountains Are Formed

Some mountains are formed when the surface of the earth is pushed up into big folds, or pieces of land. This is a very slow process that happens over millions of years. As mountains are being formed, they are also being worn down by **erosion**. This means that, over time, wind and rain wear away some of the dirt and rocks on a mountain's surface.

Some mountains are volcanoes. A volcano forms when hot rock from deep inside the earth pushes its way to the surface. This is a very fast way for a mountain to be created. A volcano can form a whole new mountain in just a few days.

Mountains and volcanoes can form whole islands that rise up from the bottom of the sea. The islands of Hawaii are made of volcanoes. The island in this picture is also a volcano.

Mountain Weather

As you climb toward the top of a mountain, the air gets colder, and there is less **oxygen**. Mountaintops can be very windy, and they are often covered in mist and clouds.

The Tree Line

As you climb a mountain, the plants become smaller. On tall mountains there is a clear height at which trees stop growing. This is called the tree line. Above the tree line, it is too cold and windy for trees to **survive**.

Alpine Flowers

The area above the tree line is called the **alpine** zone. Lots of small plants and flowers grow here. They grow close to the ground to **avoid** the cold wind.

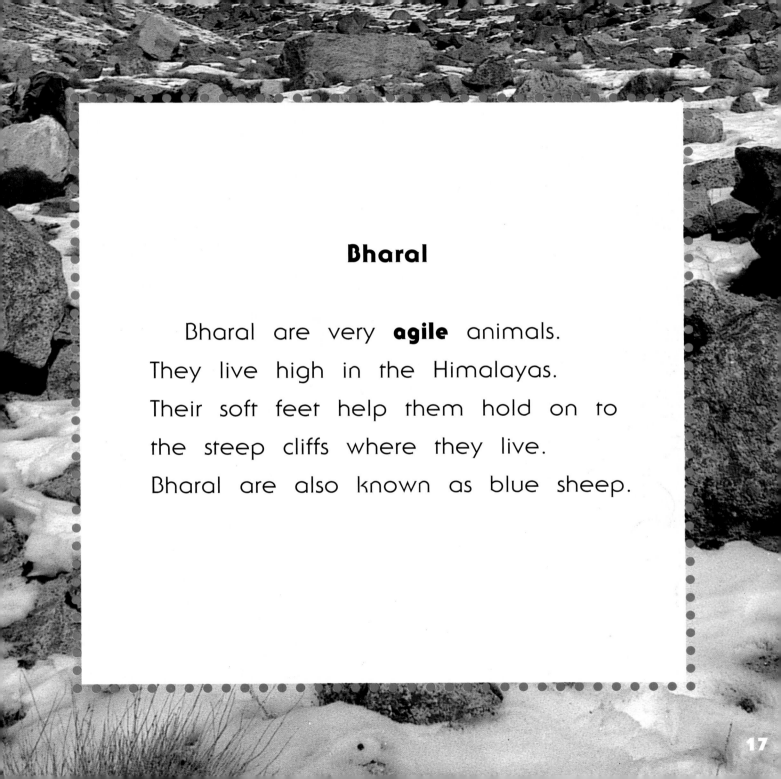

Bharal

Bharal are very **agile** animals. They live high in the Himalayas. Their soft feet help them hold on to the steep cliffs where they live. Bharal are also known as blue sheep.

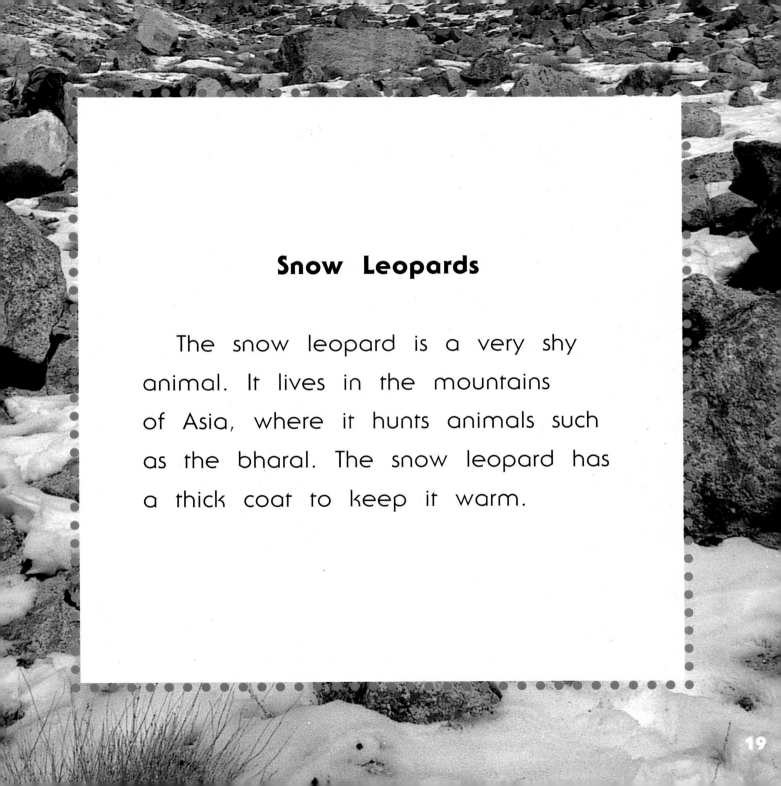

Snow Leopards

The snow leopard is a very shy animal. It lives in the mountains of Asia, where it hunts animals such as the bharal. The snow leopard has a thick coat to keep it warm.

Keas

The kea is found only in New Zealand. It is sometimes called the mountain parrot. Most parrots live in hot **tropical** forests, but keas live high up in cold mountains. A kea uses its strong beak as well as its feet to walk around in the snow.

Adapting to Mountain Life

Mountains are often covered in snow. Mountain climbers need warm clothing and special **equipment** to safely climb to the **peaks**. Plants and animals must adapt to mountain life.

GLOSSARY

agile: Able to climb and move

alpine: Belonging to or from the mountains

avoid: To stay away from something

equipment: Things that are designed for a purpose

erosion: The wearing away of dirt and rock by the weather

oxygen: The part of the air that we use when we breathe

peaks: Mountaintops

survive: To stay alive

tropical: The parts of the world that are near the equator

INDEX